Malcolm X

A Photo-Illustrated Biography
by Lucile Davis

Content Consultant:
Joanna Banks, Education Specialist
Anacostia Museum, Smithsonian Institution

Bridgestone Books

an imprint of Capstone Press

Facts about Malcolm X
- Malcolm X's name at birth was Malcolm Little.
- He was elected president of his eighth grade class.
- He preached against racism and wanted African people to work together.
- He was killed in 1965 in New York City.

Bridgestone Books are published by Capstone Press
818 North Willow Street, Mankato, Minnesota 56001 • http://www. capstone-press.com
Copyright © 1998 by Capstone Press • All rights reserved • Printed in the United States of America

Library of Congress Cataloging-in-Publication Data
Davis, Lucile.
　　Malcolm X: a photo-illustrated biography/by Lucile Davis.
　　p. cm.
　　Includes bibliographical references and index.
　　Summary: A biography of the Black Muslim who became a leader of a movement to unite black people throughout the world.
　　ISBN 1-56065-571-2
　　1. X, Malcolm. 1925-1965--Juvenile literature. 2. Black Muslims--Biography--Juvenile literature. 3. Afro-Americans--Biography--Juvenile literature. [1. X, Malcolm, 1925-1965. 2. Black Muslims. 3. Afro-Americans--Biography.] I. Title.
BP223.Z8L57332　1998
320.54'092--dc21
[B]

97-10986
CIP
AC

Photo Credits
Archive Photos, 6, 12
Corbis-Bettman, cover, 4, 8, 10, 14, 16, 18, 20

Table of Contents

Early Life

Malcolm Little was born in Omaha, Nebraska, on May 19, 1925. His father was a Baptist minister named Earl Little. Malcolm's mother was named Louise. She was Earl's second wife. Malcolm had five brothers and two sisters.

Earl preached against racism. Earl told African Americans to stand up for their rights. White men tried to stop him. They set the Littles' home on fire. No one was hurt, but all their things were burned.

Earl died in an accident when Malcolm was six years old. Some people believed that white men killed him. Louise kept her family together until she became sick. Malcolm was 13 when his mother had to go to a hospital. Malcolm moved to a foster home.

Malcolm X told African Americans to stand up for their rights. Malcolm's father had preached this message as well.

Trouble at School

Malcolm started getting into trouble at school. He was moved to a detention home when he was 13. A detention home is a prison for young people. Malcolm went back to school after a few weeks. He received good grades. He was elected president of his eighth grade class.

Malcolm told a teacher that he wanted to become a lawyer. A lawyer is someone who is trained in the law. The teacher told Malcolm that African Americans could not become lawyers. This made Malcolm angry.

Malcolm went to live with his older sister Ella. Ella lived in Boston, Massachusetts. Malcolm was only 15, but he stopped going to school. He made friends with criminals. A criminal is someone who breaks the law. Malcolm started acting like his new friends. He could not keep a job.

Malcolm went to live with his sister Ella when he was 15 years old.

Hustler and Prisoner

Malcolm's sister Ella tried to help him. She found him a job. He sold sandwiches to people riding trains. He rode on the train that went from Boston to New York.

In 1941, Malcolm went to the neighborhood called Harlem in New York City. He liked the people and the excitement. He decided to stay in Harlem.

Malcolm became a hustler. A hustler is someone who makes money by cheating or breaking the law. He sold illegal drugs and worked for criminals.

Malcolm began taking drugs and carrying a gun. At age 20, Malcolm went back to Boston. He robbed houses there. The police caught him and sent him to prison.

Being in prison made Malcolm unhappy and mean. The other prisoners called him Satan. A man named Bimbi became Malcolm's friend. Bimbi talked to Malcolm about the power of education. Malcolm respected him. Malcolm began to read and study.

Malcolm learned about the power of education.

The Nation of Islam

Malcolm changed his life. He was no longer mean. He was moved to a better prison with a large library. Malcolm read many books about history and religion.

Malcolm's brother Reginald told him about a new religion for African Americans. It was called the Nation of Islam.

The Nation of Islam was led by a man called Elijah Muhammad. Elijah told African Americans to be proud. He said they should live apart from white people. He said that white people were devils.

In 1948, Malcolm began to write to Elijah. The Muslim leader wrote back. Malcolm soon became a Muslim. He changed his name from Malcolm Little to Malcolm X. The X stood for his family's unknown African name. African-American slaves lost their names when they were brought to America. A slave is a person who is owned by someone else. Long ago, people from Malcolm's family had been slaves.

The Nation of Islam was led by a man called Elijah Muhammad.

Muslim Minister

Malcolm X was let out of prison in 1952. He went to live with his brother Wilfred in Detroit. Wilfred was a Muslim, too. A Muslim is a follower of the Islam religion. Malcolm liked the Muslim way of life. He went to the Islamic temple. A temple is a church.

Malcolm soon went to Chicago to meet Elijah Muhammad. Elijah saw that Malcolm could help the Nation of Islam.

Malcolm became a minister for the Nation of Islam. A minister is a preacher. Malcolm was a good public speaker. Many people heard him speak and decided to become Muslims.

Malcolm worked hard. Within a year, he started two new temples. In 1954, he went back to New York City to lead a temple in Harlem. Malcolm met Betty Sanders there. They were married in 1958. Over the years, they had six children.

Malcolm became a minister for the Nation of Islam.

Traveling and Preaching

By 1957, Malcolm was the Nation of Islam's most respected minister. He traveled all over the United States. He gave speeches. He spoke about African-American pride.

Malcolm told African Americans to defend themselves from racism. Defend means to keep safe. He said they should use any means necessary. His words scared white people but gave African Americans hope.

Elijah Muhammad became sick. Malcolm took on more of Elijah's work. In 1962, Malcolm became the National Minister of the Nation of Islam. Other Muslim ministers did not like all the attention Malcolm received.

Malcolm wanted to spread his message. He kept studying. He read the Koran. The Koran is the holy book of Islam. Malcolm learned more about Islam. He began to disagree with Elijah Muhammad.

Malcolm traveled all over the United States. He spoke about African-American pride.

Going to Mecca

In 1964, Malcolm left the Nation of Islam. He joined the traditional Islam religion. Traditional means practiced for a long time. He planned to build a Muslim mosque in Harlem. A mosque is a traditional Islamic church.

Malcolm also made a pilgrimage to the city of Mecca in Saudi Arabia. A pilgrimage is a trip to an important religious place. Islam teaches that all Muslims should travel to Mecca. They must try to go at least once during their lives.

In Mecca, Malcolm saw Muslims of every race and from every nation. He learned more about Islam. It taught that all people should learn to get along.

Malcolm returned home. He kept preaching against racism. Malcolm started the Organization of Afro-American Unity. He wanted African people all over the world to work together.

Malcolm started the Organization of Afro-American Unity.

The Final Year

Some people were upset with Malcolm for leaving the Nation of Islam. White people were still afraid of him. His message made some people angry.

One night a bomb exploded in Malcolm's home. He and his family escaped. Malcolm's life was in danger. But he went on with his work. He traveled around the world giving speeches. He worked on a book about his life.

On February 21, 1965, Malcolm was about to give a speech in Harlem. Before he could begin, three African-American men shot him. Malcolm died.

Malcolm X was only 39 years old. He is remembered as a powerful leader. He fought racism and brought hope to African Americans. His ideas are still important.

Malcolm is remembered as a powerful leader.

Words from Malcolm X

"Without education, you're not going anywhere in this world."

From a speech by Malcolm X in New York City on May 29, 1964.

"You can't separate peace from freedom because no one can be at peace unless he has his freedom."

From a speech by Malcolm X in New York City on January 16, 1965.

"The common goal of . . . Afro-Americans is respect as human beings. . . . We can never get civil rights in America until our human rights are first restored. We will never be recognized as citizens. . . until we are first recognized as humans."

From an interview with the *Egyptian Gazette*, August 25, 1964.

Important Dates in Malcolm X's Life

1925—Born on May 19 in Omaha, Nebraska

1931—His father, Earl, dies

1942—Becomes a hustler in Harlem

1946–1952—Serves time in prison for robbery

1948—Becomes a Muslim; joins Nation of Islam; changes last name to X

1953—Becomes a Muslim minister

1954—Starts a temple in New York City

1958—Marries Betty Sanders

1962—Becomes National Minister of the Nation of Islam

1964—Leaves the Nation of Islam; makes a pilgrimage to Mecca

1965—Killed on February 21 in New York City

1997—His wife, Betty, dies in New York on June 23

Words to Know

detention home (di-TEN-shuhn HOME)—a prison for young people

hustler (HUHSS-lur)—someone who makes money by cheating or breaking the law

Islam (ISS-luhm)—the religion of Muslims, based on the teachings of the prophet Muhammad

Muslim (MUHZ-luhm)—a person who follows the religion of Islam

Nation of Islam (NAY-shuhn UHV ISS-luhm)—a form of Islam

pilgrimage (PIL-gruhm-uhj)—a trip to an important religious place

racism (RAY-siz-uhm)—the belief that one race is better than another race

religion (ri-LIJ-uhn)—a set of beliefs people follow

Read More

Collins, David. *Malcolm X: Black Rage*. New York: Dillon Press, 1992.

Rummel, Jack. *Malcolm X*. New York: Chelsea House, 1989.

Shirley, David. *Malcolm X: Minister of Justice*. New York: Chelsea Juniors, 1994.

Useful Addresses and Internet Sites

The Institute of Islamic Information and Education
P.O. Box 41129
Chicago, IL 60641-0129

Malcolm X Institute of Black Studies
Wabash College
P.O. Box 352
Crawfordsville, IN 47933-0352

Malcolm X Archive
http://members.aol.com/jcobain/malcolmx.htm
Events and People in Black History
http://www.ai.mit.edu/~isbell/HFh/black/bhist.html

Index